BE A SHARK

Inject Self Belief, Develop Self Discipline and Start taking actions

Written by
Niall MacMillan

Table of Contents

1. Why this book

One of the things I have found over the years of my self-development journey are things that once felt unimaginable or unattainable are a lot simpler than you think. A lot closer in your reach.

Sometimes the only difference between being able to do something and to not, is just the decision you make. The story you tell yourself.

Many things put us off from trying something. Whether that be the concern of someone's opinion. The idea that someone may judge you. You would feel like a fraud, that you're not capable or you're not the type of person to do the things you've always thought of doing.

I was the same. I wasn't a gym person. I wasn't someone who could take part in physical challenges. I wasn't someone who could be a wrestler. I wasn't someone who could write a book!

There is the great Nelson Mandela quote.
"It always seems impossible until it's done."

When looking back at some of the things that I have achieved they all seem so easy now. However, before they were achieved, I didn't feel capable. They felt so out of reach and a massive mountain that would be a struggle to climb.

Now when I say my achievements. These are probably minuscule in the scheme of things. I haven't had a multi-million-dollar company. I haven't achieved a knight hood or appeared in a film with box office success. The highest award I have ever received in life was Prom King at my school prom……and this was only down to the fact I went to the effort of wearing a kilt!

The achievements I am talking about are personal achievements, ones that have allowed me to feel that I have tasted success. Not success in the eyes of others but success within myself.

This is the most important success you should strive for. Not what society or Instagram posts deem as successful. Money, Houses, Cars or Veneers, but being able to be proud of yourself.

To no longer judge yourself and to know to yourself you have done a good job. This is the Success I want this book to allow you to have. Freedom from people's opinions, freedom from judgement and most importantly freedom from yourself and your limiting beliefs.

So here are the list of my achievements..... (Get ready to be uninspired)

Achievements

Father
Husband
Website/Graphic Designer
Active Gym Member
5k Inflatable Assault Course Finisher
Tough Mudder 2017 Finisher
Three Peak Challenge Finisher
DJ
Wrestler
Podcaster (x2)
Social Media Creator
And now.........Author

Ok great.....not that amazing right....to me, this list, I am incredible proud of. I look at it and feel a great sense of worth.

Every one of the things on that list came with its own challenges and obstacles. Every one of the things on that list came with self-doubts and overthinking.

The biggest obstacle throughout each one of those on that list was myself, and the limiting beliefs that I once held at a point in time. But trust me. Once you conquer yourself.....the rest is smooth sailing.

With everything on your achievements list, once you've completed, they seems so easy. Challenge conquered; achievement gained.

With every challenge complete, you get a bigger glimpse of what is possible. You look for the next challenge and its naturally bigger than the last.

Now, it gives me great pleasure to add Author to the list. Just like the other achievements. Once this book is published, I will look back and think, well that was attainable, I am capable of that.
What's the next challenge?

Now you may think that sounds arrogant, but trust me this what I have learnt and this is what I want this book to express. Every time you achieve, it opens you up to achieve more. It exposes you to achieve bigger and better things.

I see it like a video game. Those playing a game like Call of Duty, Animal Crossing or even Candy Crush. As you progress, as you complete challenges. You unlock bigger and better things. Better levels, better weapons to use at your disposal and new abilities. You get better with each thing you unlock and before you know it, you're thriving.

You can even look at it like the movie The Matrix. (Getting the analogies in early doors!) The main character Neo, after 'beginning to believe' simply decides what skill he wants to learn. Gets a hard drive plugged into him and has the skilled uploaded.

One minute he doesn't know martial arts....... two seconds later, a quick upload....... bam......he is now an expert. Now unfortunately the pace at which we achieve this is a lot slower, however see yourself as a character, what do you want your character to be able to do. What skills do you want your character to have? Then build your character one skill at time.

Each new skill is an upgrade or something you have unlocked in your game. The game we are playing is life. You have to realise you can take control and play on your own terms or let others play the game for you.

Am I an author? I got two Cs in English GCSEs.....I have never 'published' anything in my life.....I often spell things incorrectly. I am sure you will spot them, my mum is proof reading the sh*t out of this book so if you spot them....... it's now on her!

I got told by someone at school that I had trouble tracking words and reading lines when reading. I got given some pink transparent piece of plastic to look through as an assist in my reading. Safe to say that that never got used. Can't have a pimply adolescent teen going through his tender days of school with a pink sheet for page reading!
Point being, academically I have nothing against my name to suggest I should even attempt to be author. It would be very easy to not attempt writing a book. No one could blame me.

However here I am and here you are reading my published book. This is what I want to celebrate and this is the whole purpose of the book. I am a bog-standard bloke; I am nothing special and I have no credentials to be an author but here I am doing it anyway. It's time for you to strip yourself of your limiting beliefs. Remove the anchor and get f*cking sailing.

The only thing I truly hold and hog is a truck load of self-belief. This could be down to good parenting but I like to think the majority of which has been developed from within and the people I surround myself with. I want to install the same program I have wired internally to ensure you have your own endless supply of self-belief.

I've decided to write this book for the following reasons:

A. To summarise the world of self-development. There are so many concepts within the self-development "space" and I want this book to summarise the concepts. Remove the bullshit and be a solid introduction to people new into the space.

B. To highlight, just because nothing suggests you can, doesn't mean you can't. It literally is just a decision you need to make, with yourself and hopefully by the end of this book you will be clearer on who you want to become and what you want to achieve.

C. For this book to be a repository for people to turn to when they need a helping hand. A slither of motivation. A mindset adjustor if you will. I want this book to steer people back on the right paths to help them keep momentum or kickstart them into action.

2. Self Help Space

So since embarking into the big wide world of the self-help space.....I have exposed myself to a lot. Some things that have worked great, somethings that have been a huge waste of time and somethings that sound as out there as they come but once some logic is behind it.....doesn't seem so crazy as originally thought.

So, within this first chapter I what to expose you to the three categories that exist with the 'Self Help Space'

First of all,.......

The Hustle

This I am sure you probably have all seen in your lifetimes, it's shoved in your face in social media and the people who adopt the 'Hustle' mentality normal like to shout it from the rooftops or sometimes directly in your face. All depends on the amount of caffeine, cocaine or steroids the individual has had.

The hustlers are the ones who claim sleeping is not an option. When everyone sleeps you work! Your body can survive on 4 hours sleep! Plenty of time to sleep when your dead.

I naturally think of these individuals as characters from the Wolf of Wall Street. It's all sharp suits, fancy watches and how much money they can make without any regard to other individuals. To them its dog eat dog, and they normal post quotes with lions, a set of car keys or a fancy watch on their Instagram.

Second of all......

Spiritual

Stones, star signs, 11:11 and the Universe.

These ones tend to keep themselves to themselves, because when they do share, they normally get funny looks or thought of as some sort of hippie with problems.

They believe in a higher power or a non-visible energy that steers everything.

And Last of All......

PMA

POSTIVE MENTAL ATTITUDE

These are the ones that tend to make you want to punch them in their stupid smiley faces. The ones that don't see any bad in anything. They tend to be fearful of confrontation and turn every shit situation into a magic fairy-tale where we all live happily ever after.

They will have their dogs put down and still be like "PMA!!.....Positive Mental Attitude.

Now before you feel like I have judged or labelled you. I pretty much have adopted all of the above at some point in my own self-development journey. Which is why I have no problem poking fun at myself and the stereotypes to come with the self-help world.

I have posted multiple Instagram posts in the past boasting about how much I have hustled; how much harder I have worked than others. Simple thing is though, no one gives a shit and if I'm honest it was only because I was trying to convince myself that I was getting the work done.

I have tried to push and share any spiritual beliefs I have onto others and quickly learnt that doing so just makes you sound like an absolute nut job to most. I have soon learnt that it is not up to me to change someone else's mind but to concentrate in my own beliefs and not be steered by others opinions on them.

I have also had months where I had adopted a PMA. A face that appeared to have Botox. Where nothing bad could ever happen. I could have broken an arm and still be smiling like a damn Cheshire cat!

Those are the categories.....it's not a case now of which one you should you adopt it's a case of .....where do I fit in all of this?

Somewhere in the middle

I believe there are aspects of each you should adopt to help rewire you're brain and help you have a more balanced approach to your journey to success.

Think about professional football players. Rather than just being a right footed football player and neglecting their left. They train their left to give them a better all-round game.

A sandwich would be pretty shit with just bread. You need more ingredients. Different approaches on how to motivate yourself. Discipline yourself and believe in yourself. Approaches of which I will be discussing in this book.

Approaches that will assist you in.....being a shark.

With this book, I'm not telling you what to do and saying its gospel. I'm sharing what I do and how I work on myself. With the hope you can take something from it and adapt it to your day to day.

What I have developed for myself is a formula. A repetitive pattern that with little adaptions from time to time allow me to perform at a level that I am happy with each day. Not for anyone else but for me.

The intention of the book is to help you tweak, develop and understand the formula in which you perform each day. Whether you know it or not, you have a formula, a repetitive pattern. A routine that has led to exactly where you are now.

With minor adjustments and a better understanding. You can perform a achieve more then you every thought possible each day.

The book will leave you with a formula of growth. Where you will challenge yourself each day in some capacity.

Whatever you do today, beat it tomorrow. Today's ceiling is tomorrows floor.

Whatever you're looking to achieve and whatever you're looking to become you need to apply growth and start now because whatever you have in your locker right now is not enough and it won't get you where you want to be.

Woah bit harsh Niall…..looking to feel better about myself not feel shitter…. But it's true! Let's get it out of the way early.

If you really want to achieve you have to be realistic and honest with yourself. Don't get complacent.

You need to do so much more and keep growing because I guarantee, if you got everything you wanted land in your lap today. You wouldn't feel good enough. You'd feel like you don't deserve it.

There is a reason so many lottery winners end up messed up and/or broke. You have to earn success.

You need to suffer the setbacks, suffer the daily tests and the constant struggles because when you do achieve it you will know why. You will know it's because of the new formula you've applied. You will know it's because you have grown to feel good enough to deserve the rewards.

In fact when you get what you once desired so much, you will be like……..well I deserved this……..what else can I get……and before you know it, you will be convinced that whatever you set your mind to you will get. With your formula. You can achieve anything.

3. Be A Shark

So, if you're reading this. You are obviously aware of the title. You could be forgiven if you read the title and weren't instantly convinced on what this book is about.

It's either that or you're incredible naïve and think I'm going to turn you into a one of the most dangerous fish and predators on the planet. If you're reading this and that is your current expectation, Its best we get this out of the way early. Put the book down and seek psychiatric help immediately.

You're first thought when reading the title probably was……right………well what's the message? How is being a metaphoric shark going to help me with my life and my goals?

Well this is the chapter where I explain it all.
In my previous chapter I mentioned Instagram graphics with a lion and a motivational post. However there is one other animal that is even more predominate on these cliché motivational posts…..you guessed it Sharks. Potentially one of the deadliest predators on the planet.

You give a shark a pair of lungs and set of arms and legs to match.... we're f*cked.

Now that is an opinion.....I will never claim to be a anything close to clued up on sharks. Any knowledge I hold on them I acquired from films such as Jaws and Deep Blue Sea.

Ok thanks for letting us know you barely know anything about sharks......why the hell is this book called Be a Shark then?

Being an advocate of self-development, I find it humiliating and quite honestly ridiculous that people would post a motivational quote with a graphic of a shark. How is that gonna help anyone, why the f*ck would we ever aspire to be a shark?

A shark doesn't have bills. A shark wasn't put on a 11-month lockdown because of Covid. Has a Shark ever had to put together an Ikea flat pack? Absolutely not!

I find the concept of it absolutely ridiculous and for an over a year now I have developed the phrase of 'being a shark'. Not because I am suggesting to be like a shark but because I identify it as a tongue in cheek way of expressing motivation.

It has been a way for me to share any knowledge I have picked up along my journey without people thinking that what I am saying is gospel.

Everything I share within this book and what I share on social media is what works for me, it is a way of thinking that I hold that, I believe if shared could benefit others. I don't hold any accreditation that says that what I have written in this book or I what I do share has any weight.

It's my nod of expression that although I'm sharing advice. I'm still on a learning journey myself and I'm not taking myself too seriously like I'm some sort of w*nky life guru.

Truth be told I f*cking hate sharks. I remember after watching Jaws I feared baths and took part in a fair amount of apprehensive poos for a few weeks....... as if a shark was gonna get me on the toilet!

What I want 'Be a Shark' to be identified by is a way of believing in yourself, do what you can and then strive for more. There is a heap of sh*t out there in the motivational world that doesn't get down to the brass taxes of things.

How we can live a life filled with the standard unfair obstacles most face but while striving to not just keep our head above water but to test ourselves and achieve more than most, to strive for more and constantly looking for ways to improve ourselves.

A lot of us leave school and think the learning stops there. We know we will have to learn in a job, learn to be a parent, learn to be an adult but in terms of working on your own skill sets, and being a student.

Majority of us stop. We are never taught in school and it is never really preached to us that the learning should never stop. Being a Shark means to constantly look for areas for upgrade.

It's to look at your last year as version 6.2 of yourself and look to become 7.0 the next year. What are we going to accomplish now? What bigger and better things are we now going to take on.

We've all updated our phone and noticed new features and abilities. We should be looking to constantly upgrade and add new features to ourselves often. It's no surprise so many people feel at a dead end or lost. We not reminded to constantly look to better ourselves. So many people are standing still and settling. For us to live life to the fullest we must continually look for ways to improve. Never settle.

Let's face it.....we're all whinging it, none of us truly know what we are doing. At whatever age you are reading this. You don't get to an age and stop having life throw you curveballs. Why not have a book that potentially can help us along the way.

So, what does it mean to Be a Shark?

Be a Shark means to belief in yourself, do what you can and then push to strive for more. Don't take yourself and your shit to seriously and when an obstacle rears its ugly head. Recognise it for what it is, a temporary obstacle that we can overcome with the sharky ways instilled throughout this book.

Being a Shark is about taking the action, even on the days we don't feel like it. It's about winning the battles we have inside our own heads and relentless looking for self love and self improvement every single day. Not settling, not staying comfortable and pushing on to get the most out of your time.

Get it? Makes sense?......right now let's tackle our first obstacle.....completing this book and being a f*cking shark!

4. Happiness

It's what we all seek, happiness, inner peace. It's the main objective in life.

For a lot of people its money, its accolades, its raising children, it's being remembered for something. It's sitting back eating a pizza watching Schitts Creek on Netflix.

Happiness is success

People think they will be happy when they have lots of money, when they have nice things, when they're important.

Money cannot buy you happiness. You've heard that old saying. Well it really is true.

When you actively pursue money, your happiness is no longer a priority. Your sacrificing it for a small piece of paper (or plastic these days). Hoping to suffer enough but to earn enough to be happy in the future. Its ridiculous. You can be happy now.
Why would you need a certain amount to make you happy?

Pursue happiness, make it a task every day to wake up every morning positively and end everyday with your head on your pillow content.

The most ironic thing is. When you pursue happiness when you make happiness your priority the money and the nice things gravitate towards you anyway. Without working too hard to achieve them.

Take some time to think about what truly makes you happy, not what society tells you makes you happy. What makes you feel giddy. What makes you feel alive?

Then when you have this, no questions asked. Without hesitation. Seek it every day.

When it comes to seeking happiness, we need to be selfish. We need to think only of our own happiness. Why waste all our energy trying to please others.

A lot of people, mainly mothers feel guilty doing this. Like nature intended, they dedicate their lives to their children and the raising of their kids.

The idea of being 'Selfish' and thinking only about themselves is foreign to them.

There is the oxygen mask principle. When you are instructed on how to use an oxygen mask on an airplane you are told to ensure you apply your own oxygen mask first.

This is because you will be better suited to help the others around you if you have secured your oxygen first.

Putting yourself first doesn't mean you don't care about others. It means you're smart enough to know you can't help others if you don't help yourself first.

With myself I found myself going to work, coming home, getting in front of my TV and gaining weight. I had goals but took no action, I had no growth and dedicated myself to being Dad. Work, Provide and Be there. That was my life.

Whilst I was fulfilling the duties of being a Dad, I was a very miserable one. I was short with my wife, grumpy and would fly off the handle for any small thing. Mainly due to the lack of sleep.

I wasn't making myself a priority and although I wasn't taking 'selfish' time to myself I was being selfish because I wasn't giving my wife and daughter the Dad I wanted to be or they deserved.

Once I learnt my second child, my first son was on his way. I knew something had to change.

What I started to do was dedicate 1-2 hours each morning entirely to myself. I would set my alarm for half 5 and go to the gym. Nothing crazy but just jump on a cross trainer, mid resistance for half an hour and then walk back with some sort of self-development podcast and or audiobook. Something that makes me think and learn from.

I would serve myself early before life even begun, before the day even started. When I returned home. I was awake, I was aware, I was present and in a fantastic mood. What I started to realise was it was because I dedicated the time to working on myself.

I would seek discomfort early and I achieve what I set out to do early. Doing this has incredible mental benefits. It clears the headspace and took so much stress off my mind. Let alone all the scientific health benefits of endorphins, increase of oxygen levels and all that shit.

I can't tell you how amazing it feels to tick two or three things off the to do list before the day has even starts. The rest of the day becomes easy and you're better prepared for what other unexpected shit life has to throw at you.

Now, if anything I am far more selfish. I dedicate the morning hours to myself. I invest in myself financially with materials/courses that will help me level up. I trained once a twice a week for 2 years to fulfil on of my life goals of being a wrestler. I took part in numerous runs, climbs and events. I ensured pure personal growth and I still do it daily.
This may still sound to selfish but now my family have a Dad who knows who he is, knows what he wants, a Dad that holds self-belief and self-worth, a

Dad who is fit enough to play and mess around with them. A dad who is truly happy.

I am truly happy because I worked hard to get to this point. I am a much better parent. Many parents tell their kids how to do things in life, and teach through words. I look to teach my kids by showing them how to achieve in life with my actions.

I'm sure as a parent you want your child to hold self worth, self-belief, a desire to learn, a desire to grow and a desire to be the best version of themselves they can be. You want your kids to be truly happy.

How could you possibly preach that to your kids when you hold none of those values yourself?
Make yourself a priority. Look after yourself. Look after your body, look after your mind.
Being selfish allows you to:

- Be more confident.
- Be more self-resilient.
- Take ownership
- Ensure Growth

Even as a couple, as much as I think it's important to make each other happy. I think its much better for each person in a relationship to work to achieve their own happiness selfishly and share the happiness they have with each other selflessly, rather than one partner being depended on to manage the others moods. Both people in a relationship should look to work on themselves and enjoy the spoils together.

Success/Happiness is achieving any goals that you give yourself. Not anyone else's goals. Your goals, the ones you set yourself. Whether they are long term goals, short term goals or even little daily ones.

Inner success is not letting the little voice in your head win. Not giving in to it, not giving up, but achieving what you set out to do. Aiming to do that at all levels and looking to do it every day.

Settling for less than what you deserve is not true happiness. Settling because you don't think you're good enough is not true happiness.
Settling for less than you deserve because of others judgement or opinions is not true happiness.

Living your live how you want to. Doing the things that make you feel alive, make you feel good about yourself is true happiness.

Being truly happy in your own skin, being truly comfortable and content with yourself. Celebrating what you have and what you offer unapologetically is the happiness and success we should all be seeking.

You're gonna have plenty days where you're not gonna believe in yourself, plenty of days where you don't feel good enough. I'm here to tell you, that it's a choice you are making. You own the narrative. It is you who can decide how you want to live you life and what story you want to be part of. You are the outcome of the story you tell yourself in your head.

My purpose with this book is remind you that you are worth so much more than you think. You are capable of so much and I want nothing but success for you.

It's time for you to think of you, it's time for you to take control, stand up and take what's yours……it's time for you to BE A SHARK!!

Wow……even I'm pumped up…. see it's the perfect cheesy motivational line. Now let's crack on with the book!

5. Your Why

Why do you go to work? Why do you live the life you lead? What is your reason to jump out of bed?

What is your Why statement?

Don't worry, if you haven't thought of one yet. Majority of us let our day to day lives lead us into understanding our purpose. Dictate our why. But have you ever stopped for a second and thought about what you really want, what you want to achieve? Why your current job or lifestyle isn't helping you get the results you want? Does it adhere to your why?

What is a why statement?

Your "Why" statement is a statement of purpose that describes why you take the actions you do, the work you do and the life you lead.

If you feel unmotivated, lost or unfulfilled, it is because you most likely don't have a clear understanding of your "why".

You could be living someone else's why or just winging shit month after month letting life steer your why.

Before you know it, you are in a job that doesn't satisfy you, you're doing things that you don't actually enjoy and you feel lost and alone.

Having a 'Why' gives you back control. It helps you evaluate the things around you, to ensure they are living up to your why, to your standard. It gives you a purpose.

Having a purpose, helps you stay focused, gives your something to be passionate about, gives you a sense of integrity.

I will give you two examples of people who potential need to learn or re-evaluate their why:

The School Leaver

Meet Jamie – Jamie currently works in office as a junior chartered accountant. Jamie originally wanted to work as videographer, but his friend got him a job at his company and has been told there is good money in accounting.

He currently earns good enough money to help pay for his car that he got on finance and have enough money to go out with his friends once a week. He has saved a bit each month as he eventually knows he is going have to buy a house and move out but nowhere near enough.

He won't me moving out for a least 17 years at this rate. His current why (whether he knows it or not) is to make the most money he can in a job he doesn't enjoy and live for the weekend with his friends.

His why is short term and it keeps him happy until the Monday morning alarm goes off and he starts again.

Fast forward 6 years. Jamie, still without his why, has met and married his wife. He has become a Senior Chartered accountant. He has 2 kids and lives in a good sized 3 bed house.

Jamie goes to work each day to a well-paid job, he comes home, sits in front of the tv every night. Puts his kids to bed each night, does something family orientated each weekend. Repeat.

Jamie has what society deems as everything he should have. He is married, he has a lovely family and earns enough money to live comfortably and contribute into society.

However, Jamie, feels flat, Jamie is unhappy. He has everything he thought he wanted/needed and now feels guilty, as he doesn't feel happy.

He doesn't feel fulfilled. Jamie's why is still earning good enough money doing a job he doesn't enjoy to live for the weekend. He is living each day, each week, each month on repeat. Before you know it, a few years go by and he is 29. Overweight, miserable, lazy and unhappy.

The Mom

Second Example – Meet Sarah

Sarah is a Mum of two beautiful kids. She has been married for 5 years. Her husband has a highly paid engineering job which keeps him at away from home most days a week.

Both kids are now in school so Sarah now has some time to herself during the day. Sarah responsibilities mostly lie with the children.

Feeding them, getting them ready for school, taking them to and from school etc.

Sarah's why – she is a mum. This is how she identifies herself and feels she isn't not being a good enough 'Mum' if she didn't.

Sarah finds herself binge watching Netflix and snacking in-between wash loads during the day and having a glass of wine each night to get over the 'Day' she has had. (Which by the way, there is nothing wrong with!)

With her why and her purpose being solely 'Mum'. She is putting everyone around her first. Rather than herself. Whilst noble, Sarah eventually loses her identity and purpose. She loses touch in who she is and suffers from a lack of Motivation.

Both Sarah and Jamie, without having a strong grasp on their why both feel lost and suffer a lack of confidence and motivation.

They no longer feel in control and their lives end up being dictated by others for them.

Introducing and understanding their why will help give them a purpose, inner confidence, control and a direction.

Your Sat Nav

You have just booked a trip to the Lake District for a getaway, you have a nice cottage booked for the week. You have decided to drive. You're are all packed and ready to go.

What's one of the first things you do when setting off on your journey? You set your sat nav. You put in the destinations postcode and away you go.

You set off on your journey, knowing that your path is laid out in front of you and all you have to do is follow it.

You know that if there is any unexpected hiccups, your sat nav is either going to keep you on the same path or give you a slight diversion. However still taking you and leading you to your final destination.

Imagine this journey without a sat nav. Without a route in mind. It's not gonna be a fun journey. You will be stressing out, doubting yourself and struggling to get where you want to.

Now imagine if you didn't have a cottage already booked. Imagine you didn't have a predetermined destination in mind? You would be driving blindly down a multitude of roads. Hoping to reach a destination that is good enough to satisfy your needs. You could be driving hours and hours only to end up at a destination that 'will do' but not one that you would have chosen.

Inside all with us we have an inner compass. An inner sat nav. This works without you even realising. It's called your sub conscious.

If your why is clear, if your destination is clear. You can relax and trust in your sub conscious to make the right decisions, take the right turns and divert your when necessary.....but overall you can trust it that all the decisions, turns and diversions are with your final destination in mind.

When you have inner navigation.....even when you deviate slightly from your path temporarily. You still have your end goal in mind and you know the paths you need to get back on course to continue towards your goals.

This can remove stress, increase self-belief with a knowing that you're on your way. When having your why you will soon notice the people around you without their why. Lost and bumbling around trying to find a place that 'will do' rather than the place they desire.

When you have a strong why, the inner navigation is managed by you and your self-conscious. When somebody offers you something, if somebody asks something of you...your inner sat nav can quickly process, see if it fits in with your why and your goals. If it doesn't then you can reject. If it does then you can accept. This is instantaneous. This is without even umming and awing. It starts managing your decision process without even having to really think.

Build your why

So how to build you why? What we want to do is build yourself a Mission statement. Let's get an idea of your end destination, the goals you want to achieve and the routes you want to take.

Use the 5 statements and see how it fits in for you. Feel free to fill in the gaps. Make it real.

What makes you feel more like you?

When you are gone, what do you want to be remembered by?

What are your strengths, the one that make you feel great?

What would a young you want and are you doing it?

What would you regret not doing?

6. Self-Belief

This chapter I want to talk about Self Belief and why the buck stops with you.

Where ever you are in life. The current situation you are in.....it is your fault.

It is not your bosses' fault, it's not your partner or ex-partners fault, it's not your friends' fault, it's not your parents' fault, it's not your teachers fault......it's not the card you were dealt's fault. It is entirely your fault!

Once again, may seem a bit harsh but it's true.

The only person who can change the situation you are in is you. Do not blame anyone else.

When you take full ownership of your problems you take back your control. You relinquish it from anyone else. When the buck stops with you, then you know it's up to you to change things.

The word 'self' is in 'self belief' for a reason, it is entirely up to you.

If you're in a relationship where you are unhappy, where you lack confidence, drive and self-belief. It would be easy to blame your partner but this is something you need to fix.

Although it's nice for a partner to assist they really can't be depended on to solve your problems. The same way you wouldn't expect them to depend on you completely for theirs. They have their own belief issues going on. Why should they worry about your self-belief?

If you feel like you're being held back from work, feel you are unhappy and in a dead-end job. Whose fault is that? Not your bosses. It's yours. First of all, would you promote and have confidence in someone for a role if they didn't have enough self-belief and confidence within themselves. Why take the risk? You wouldn't. Get to work believing in yourself then people will start to believe in you.

If you are unhappy in your work, don't enjoy what you're doing? Is that your bosses' fault, is it your colleagues' fault? You already know the answer.

If you have experienced something in your past that wasn't deserved. Your past has now put you in a position where you can't get on with life? Is this your pasts fault? Don't give your past too much weight.

Some people have more passion about their past then their future.

If you think of yourself as a plant and the only one responsible for watering you is yourself? What state would you be in? Would you be a great big green beauty? Standing tall and strong? Or would you be a little scraggly thing that stinks up the joint, surrounded by those little shitty muggy fruit flies?

Time to get the watering can!

Your responsible for your own life. You're entirely in control.

No One Cares!

Now what I learnt to realise back in the day and took me a while to get my head around is……No One cares!

What do I mean?......I mean whatever it is you're trying to do to improve yourself…..no one gives a shit.

Do not expect motivation or intense level of care from anyone else.

Why should anyone care that you're going to try and work on you?
Why should anyone care that you're trying to lose weight? Why does anyone care that you want to take up a new hobby?

Why should anyone care that you're going to stop being an easy lay now and going to try to have more respect for yourself???

Truly, no one gives a shit! Bit demoralising? Don't let it be. Understand that this is the reality of it. Don't expect anything of anyone else apart from yourself. Any care that you do get (probably from your parents) is a bonus!

People have plenty of their own shit going on, their own little journeys that they are navigating themselves through.

Think about all the thoughts you have throughout the day. Think of the thoughts you are having now. Those are your thoughts from your perspective. You are the main character in your own story. How can you expect to be the main character in someone else's story? Everyone is main event in their own heads.

So, when it comes to you starting out on your little 'Self Dev' journey, don't be put out that you don't get messages from people saying you go girl! You can do it mate! Do not improve yourself for the wrong reasons, don't improve yourself for someone else.

Improve yourself entirely and only for you're own benefit. When you truly belief in yourself, others will benefit from it and the thought of no one caring about you and what you do doesn't even hit the sides, if anything it empowers you!

Motivation isn't everything!

Now another reason why you can't depend on other people for your journey. Other people with their support can help increase motivation. Being part of a social group, having a tight group of supportive friends. They can really help support and boost you when you're feeling low on motivation.

Motivation is great.....when you have it....however it comes and goes like a wave. Your friends aren't gonna be there all the time to motivate you. You won't also have someone when your motivation is low.

You won't always have someone to close the fridge when you're going for that late-night snack. You won't have someone yanking you out of bed when you set your alarm for 6am to get up and go gym.

Motivation is not the key to keeping at something and staying on target. The key is Discipline!

Not as sexy I know. Sounds a bit army base as well doesn't it. However, discipline, if worked on and installed is your little firewood and matches. It is your catalyst to create your own motivation. Discipline is your magic bean!

When there are mornings when I don't wanna move out of bed. Moments when I just don't fancy it. (There are plenty for me!) I don't depend on my motivation.....I depend on discipline.

When you have those lazy/low moments....and we all have them! Where you know you gotta do something but really can't be arsed.... Do it anyway!

When use your discipline and do it anyway it generates a whopping great big dose of motivation. More motivation then if you DID actually feel like doing the task and doing it anyway.

It's another hack and one I highly promote.

In the army, and I experienced this back in my days in the cadets. You're made to polish your boots and told to fold your bed in a particular way each day. Then inspected on it! I remember thinking how is this helping. How are my shiny boots gonna help me in a battlefield? These army folds on my duvet are not gonna wins us a war!

However, on reflection, this is a task to install discipline. Doing these tasks that no one gets excited for. Any task achieved gives you a boost. A dose of motivation. A sense of accomplishment. No matter the size of the task. Doing a task you really don't want to do gives you a bigger achievement. Doing this donkey work and making your bed in the morning is a task achieved earlier. It sets your day in a positive direction.

The one I use personally is the dishwasher. There is many a time where I open the dishwasher and notice it is full.....my soul dies a little! I end up at a crossroads.....take on the horrible mundane task of emptying it or just ignore it. Leave it for someone else or do it later.

I also have those thoughts, every damn time I open that dishwasher. However, I have learnt that I feel f**king fantastic when I take the 2 minutes of my time to get it done! It's another box ticked.

The more tasks ticked the bigger your motivation dick!

Boom! There is the book quote! Put that on a bumper sticker or Instagram post.

You are capable of so much more than you think. You, even on a good day, are only running at 40%.

You've got 60% left in the tank. Tap into that by being kind to yourself.

Don't settle for any less and have the belief that there is always more for you to achieve. Once you remove the limitations you have about yourself, you can work to achieve anything.

The way you think of yourself sometimes is 300% worse then what anyone will think of you. Just remember you're the bollocks! You are capable of so much more then what you think you deserve and you have so much to offer others!

It's ok to have doubts, its ok to feel not good enough but just remember that these thoughts are temporary. Acknowledge them and move on. Be kind to yourself and don't forget to celebrate yourself.

Talk yourself up even, I don't care if you right a sentence done and repeat to yourself in the mirror. You may feel strange at first but keep telling yourself why you're the bollocks and your sub conscious will listen, it will fall in line.

Make a list of all your positives, all your achievements and remember that so many people value you and someone out there is looking up to you.

Join them in realising how f*cking fantastic you are and make sure you don't forget it.

Believing in yourself is a constant battle. It is a battle against your mind, not anyone else. Doubt and fear of failure will constantly try to occupy your head.

You have weaknesses? You're not that good a somethings? So what. Nobody is perfect and you shouldn't be striving for perfection. That is an exhaustive endeavour. Just remember what you're amazing at and go balls deep!

Believing in yourself or self loving isn't arrogance, it just means that you believe in yourself so much, you need no other to believe in you.

Other people don't really have a say in who you will become as much as you think they do. Only you have that say. It is a decision you have to make.

Treat yourself and give yourself a better life then the one you belief you deserve.

So whether your name is Pete and you're thinking of releasing some music, or Sophie and you want to go out on your own as a lash technician.

Remember this. You are capable if you believe it for yourself. Make the decision, figure out who you are, how your mind tries to stop you, then make a stand, shock you inner voice by flipping the script and never look back.

Whether you think you can or think you can't. Your right. Believe that you can.

7. Your Formula

Every morning when we wake up, we have a pattern and a routine that we habitually follow. A lot of which you're probably not aware of. We wake up, have a stretch, rub our eyes, grab a drink, go toilet etc.....

We often do the same things before the days start, during the day and at the end of a day. Some of which that serves us and some of which doesn't'.

A daily pattern that we repeat regularly. This is your formula.

What we do daily and often determines our future. Our formula determines our level of success down the line.

A strong formula which is filled with the things that DO serve you, is effectively a blue print for what you can expect in the future.

Dead Time vs Alive Time

Now on average we all have around 15 hours a day of awake time. This could be broken down as an hour and a bit in the morning. 7-8 of work and then 4-5 at night.

Dead Time

No growth, no stress. No concept of time. Refreshing news feeds, watching TikToks, binge watching Netflix. Jumping into the warzone.

Alive Time

Investment of your time into future growth. Taking control. Being active. Being present. Working on something, planning for something or learning something new.

Now I'm not bashing Dead time at all. When people have stressful jobs, stressful kids.....dead time is 100% required. We are all allowed to relax and should find time to ourselves each day to have this downtime.

However, there are people living out their formula with no inclusion of alive time whatsoever.

If were saying work consumes 7-8 hours of work. That leaves 7 hours of free time. Let's call it 5 because you might take time to do your hair in the morning and eat your dinner when you get home.

How are you utilising the remaining 5 hours? What is your ratio of Dead/Alive time?

If you're spending 4-5 hours each night binge watching Netflix and it is part of your formula. It's not unreasonable to expect slow growth. You cannot moan at anyone when you're stuck in the same job for years and gaining weight.

Now I'm not saying not to watch Netflix, I'm not a prick! Surely 1-2 hours is enough though at worst. That's at least 6 episodes of Cobra Kai!

This leaves 2-3 hours of dead time that you can convert to Alive time.

Any increase in Alive time is only going to benefit you in the long run. You're gonna slowly build confidence in yourself and what you will notice that as you learn, as you grow you're going to gain momentum. You're going to start to feel a bit more....... alive. Funny that. Rather than being the Numb numpty living on the sofa.

So back to our Formula....

A formula, is identifying all the things that DO serve you, all the things that DO benefit you and understanding how and when they benefit you.

Colonel Sander (KFC) developed his secret recipe, his formula, with trial and error. Not only did he identify what ingredients he needed but when to apply them to the mixture.

You may already know that going for a half hour walk benefits you each day. However, going in the morning may make you late for work. You may find that you can't really be bothered at the end of the day. It actually may be better for you to take a quick half hour on your lunch break to your favourite lunch spot.

A strong formula includes your alive and dead time. But its important to understand your utilisation of both throughout the day. Each person is going to be different.

There is no right or wrong time of when to apply the Dead/Alive time. Whatever time best suits you. This is why it's your formula.

My formula includes 2 hours of alive time each morning before work and before the kids wake up. This includes exercise, listening to an audiobook or working on a personal project. Then half hour each night for creating a goofy TikTok.....maybe an hour and a half if I'm really struggling. This is what works for me.

You may be more of a night owl. You may like to break your alive time up through the day.

But if there is one thing you take from this chapter. It's up your alive time! Without alive time......there is little to no growth. It's as simple as that.

Stop wasting your own time procrastinating doing pointless shit. You know exactly the stuff I'm talking about. Apply some more Alive time and actually feel more Alive

Get your finger out of you arse and start living, start getting stuff done. Doesn't matter who you are or what your situation is, there is dead time that we can eliminate throughout the day.

Do you want to be asked on your death bed if you have any regrets? Do you want sit there sad and whimpering stringing of a list of regrets? Or do you want to want smile back and say 'Fuck no!' on your dying breath!

Amend your formula! Decrease the deadtime and increase the alive time.

X = Alive Time
Y = Dead Time
Z = Fulfilment

X-Y = Z!

Formula Bitches!

8. Autopilot

Do you ever sit in the car and get to your destination and stop to think......how the hell did I even get here! You don't remember taking the turns. You don't remember going around the roundabouts. Stopping at the red lights.

Your head was so far away and you realise you wasn't even truly 'there' with your driving. This is autopilot, where you've driven the same route so much you don't even really need to concentrate.

You're almost programmed, the route and the motions are so ingrained our brains we have developed a decision-making system that does the work for you......it just happens. It's almost like somebody else is doing the driving for us.

This takes place in plenty other areas of our life's as well. Just not as life threatening as doing it in a car. We autopilot with what we eat, what we watch on TV and what we wear etc...

We can wake up in the morning and before you know it, you're at work. You plod away at work and then before you know it, you're at home with a can of beer or glass of wine and a bag of something Cadbury on the sofa. None of these choices you have really made but you're autopilot has.

When you're on autopilot, time seems to drift by and its filled with mind numbing stuff that help you get you through the day safely (which is its purpose) but wouldn't you rather feel awake and alive then barely making it through a day at the bare minimum?

Signs of autopilot:

You're unhappy and unfulfilled

This is the first obvious sign. Although it is your autopilot.... it's almost like someone else is living your life for you. Everything is just so automatic. It's no surprise you start to feel unhappy. Your brain is working at the minimum rate it needs to and most days for you are forgetful. You may even wake up filled with dread because you know exactly how your day is gonna go.

La La Land

Throughout the day you constantly catch yourself drifting in and out of deep thought. Thinking about things that 30 seconds later you can't even remember.
Plenty of times a day....you find yourself never truly there.

Where did time go?

You notice time is going by so quickly but with nothing to show for it. You are living groundhog day but not getting the time back to relive. Months/Years are going by with nothing to show for it.

Overthinking

When you're drifting off in and out thought throughout the day you tend to overthink about something that hasn't happened yet. Whether it is out of fear and doubt or out of fantasy. You may fixate on your past and not truly have a hold on the present.

"To be fully alive, fully human, and completely awake is to be continually thrown out of the nest." ~Pema Chodron

Wake up!

Now I'm not talking about waking up by having a strong coffee each morning. I'm talking about getting yourself out of autopilot and start taking control of your life and making your time count.

We naturally lean towards habits and what is automatic. Make your habits ones that rattle you out of autopilot and into an active state.

Here are a number of ways to get yourself out of Autopilot

1. Task for the day

Set yourself a task for the day. It could be anything, it could be returning that parcel you have been putting of posting. Fixing those things around the house that has been bothering you. Clearing some clutter in a bedroom or cupboard.myl Buying that present for an upcoming birthday.

Although not big tasks its incredible how easy these little tasks clutter our headspace. Completing one or two a day not only clear that headspace but it gives you a great sense of achievement for the day.

Even more so when you stack a few together in one day. Having a goal for the day helps you control it and gives its purpose.

2. Organise something

Booking something for later down the road helps give you something to look forward to. Something that is exciting, something that is gonna make you feel alive. Maybe something that brings fear and adrenaline like a bungee jump or a challenge.
Book somewhere you have never been before, something you can tick of a list. Even just booking something is enough to make you start to feel like you have more control like a hair appointment that's been long overdue or a catch up meal/call with friends.

3. Be Present

The word meditation puts some people off but mediation allows you to be truly present on your current state and how you really feel for the day.

Try Sit and be still for 3-4 minutes. Concentrate solely on your breathing. Feeling your lungs fill up, holding your breath and slowly releasing. I'm not gonna try to tell you how to do it in a book but there are plenty of shorts videos easily accessible online that help you do this.

You will realise how many thoughts try to enter your mind when you're doing this. Letting them drift by and being truly present really helps gain perspective for the moment and help you out of the autopilot funk.

4. Be Human

Speak to someone you don't normally speak to, learn something about someone. Do something for someone else, a gesture for someone with no expectation of anything back. Just be real with someone, without any front and just connect by being a human with someone. It's good for heart and mind. One for the soul!

5. Shake Up

We all have habits. We go the exact same way to work, sit at the exact same table, go to the exact same coffee shop every day. Changing up this routine gives our minds a different thought and adjustment. Whether that be taking a different route, changing what you have for breakfast or learning a new skill.

it inspires us to think differently. It may be in a small way, but by changing up your routine every now and then or learning something new, you start to think more and stop the feeling of being on autopilot every day.

Life can be unpredictable and scary; coasting through without making big, meaningful changes is one way to feel a bit safer. However, that's not a way to live an exciting and fulfilling life though!

9. Uncomfortable

The one thing that I believe everyone needs to strengthen and one of the most important muscle that needs to be flexed, is your mindset. With a strong and powerful mindset, so much can be achieved.

It really is the difference maker. It what separates the normal to the successful. If social media really is this great monster people claim it is then the only true weapon against it is a strong mindset.

How would you look to become stronger? You would lift weights, eventually increasing the weight, with every increase in weight, the stronger you get. With habitual repetition and constant increase of weight and increase of the resistance to work the muscles to get stronger.

How would you lose weight? By putting your body through rigorous exercise to a point where you expend energy. To do this you have to put your body under some sort of stress.

Progress only truly comes with some level of discomfort. A shock to the system, something that just keeps the body guessing.
The same should be applied to our minds.

Naturally we all lean towards the path of least resistance. We look for the easiest and shortest route. This is the default. I'm sure if we all had the choice we would be in good shape, strong and great at our jobs with the least amount of effort.

Unfortunately, people's default mindset doesn't achieve this. We need to do uncomfortable things to see progress. Whether that be a simple task of getting the kids lunches ready, hoovering or walking the dog. Tasks that if we could get away with not doing, we wouldn't bother.

It's far too easy to apply the default and stay comfortable but without discomfort we will not see the progress. If you want to learn something, you have to do something you haven't done before. Put yourself in a position you are unfamiliar with. If you want to earn more, you need to take on more than you do and expose yourself to other responsibilities.

There will always be a voice telling you to stick to default. The same as autopilot. We need to realise the voice is there trying to make us take the safe shortcut but we should look to choose the path of most resistance. That is where the growth is and that is where you sit back at the end of the day and be proud of yourself knowing you have not avoided effort.

If you just keep doing things the same way over and over again, you'll keep getting the same results. If you don't like the results you're getting, take a new path.

Learning to be comfortable with discomfort is one of the most important skills you can ever have to live a truly fulfilling life. If you learn this skill, you can master pretty much anything.

The life we seek isn't found by avoiding pain and staying safe. It comes from contentment in knowing you've pushed the limit and you're doing exactly what you have to do to be better!

If you join the 'easy' crowd, then you will not grow. If you surround yourself with people who have settled with 'Default' then this will latch onto you like an anchor. Holding you back and keeping you in a stand still.

It's always important to surround yourself with people who push themselves because in turn they will push and inspire you with them. Strap yourself to rocket, not an anchor.

Breaking a habit, trying something new, taking a risk, making new connections, or putting yourself in a totally new situation won't be easy, but it's worth it. It's exhausting but rewarding.

When you are challenged, you are asked to become more than you were. That means creating new perspectives, acquiring new skills and pushing boundaries.

Repetition expands your comfort boundaries. If you practice your discomforts enough, with different activities, your comfort zone will expand to include discomfort.

Think about it. How many things were once uncomfortable for you which you now accept without difficulty?

Driving, how many times did you stall it or freak out on that parallel park? Was it worth the discomfort though?

Heck even walking, do you think babies sit and have doubts on whether they should bother walking after stacking it face first while trying to stand up in the kitchen? Failing is part of mastering.

A word that has been used to describe the majority of the latest Generations. Millennials and Generation Z. Are Snowflakes

Snowflakes - A very sensitive person. Someone who is easily hurt or offended by the statements or actions of others.

Now some people despise this word as it promotes people to not express opinions or vulnerabilities. I myself am not a fan of the word, as to me it just reminds me of an old man sitting in his chair going "well back in my day" scoffing at the new generation completely out of touch on how the world now works. I choose to speak about it though as I feel that I belong to that generation.

However you want to label it, whether it is Snowflakes, Wet Blanket or a Dry lunch. There are a lot of individuals who hold themselves as a victim. Who feel they are owed something. Feel they are getting the short straw. People who when they have their opinions opposed, fold like a deck chair.

Rather than taking ownership for their own circumstance they blame everyone else. They shy away from any discomfort and hide away in their 'safe space'.

How can they be blamed though? We live in a society now where things we want can come to us quite easily.

Life is the most comfortable it may have ever been, even during a global pandemic! We can get food delivered, communicate without leaving the house, we can access anything online yet some of us have grown so weak and become far too comfortable.

Everyone is looking for quick solutions. The easiest paths. The shortcuts.

Without any hard work, we can be driven from one place to another with a few taps of a screen with Uber. We can go to the supermarket and be met by an abundance of food. We can get our favourite meal delivered straight to our front door. We have access to untold amount of knowledge and can learn anything online in a device in our hands.

This I think has dampened independence. We don't have to struggle to get comfort, its handed to us.
If anything, seeking discomfort in this day and age, not looking for a shortcut and doing the hard work will get us further today than it ever would in any previous generations.

Everyone is wrapped in cottonwool, pushing your limits even a little bit each day will set you apart tenfold.

If you practice it enough, you will soon seek discomfort with most of what you do.

When you get used to discomfort and make it a habit, If one day you wake up in the morning and choose not to go to the gym, not to empty the washing machine, not to do the thing you said you would. If you woke up and chose the easy route, it will end up bothering you all day, you'll have it on your mind like a feeling of guilt.

Look to avoid that guilt by doing the uncomfortable, by doing what you said you would, by seeking the discomfort daily.

So next time you are at a cross road in your mind, look to choose the path of most resistance. Look for the discomfort and appreciate discomfort often is where the growth comes from.

10. Comparison

With Social Media nowadays it's very easy to open your phone, scroll down your news feed and instantly feel like shit.

How many hours a day are we on Social Media.... maybe an hour, maybe two? That's a lot of time spent scrolling through people's highlights.

Whether it's comparing yourself to people you know or people you have never met. Everyone's highlights are on social media now. We can see someone's post about buying a new car, their dramatic weight loss or them living it up on holiday at a luxury resort.

Seeing these highlights may triggers feelings of resentment and jealousy. Provide you with a big cloud of self-doubt that you weren't even looking for.

A lot of what is posted is exaggerated and even tactical. You are only seeing the good. None of the bad.

I have seen first-hand individuals take 40-45 mins getting the most pixel perfect picture for their

Instagram and then posting it claiming they're 'Living their best life!'.

There is plenty of bullshit and facades online to be weary of. I think a lot of us are slowly starting to see through it now. However it doesn't stop us feeling a bit shitty seeing something someone else has and thinking……I want that…..I wish I could be like that……I wish I could be that.

However Bullshit or not, comparing yourself against someone else's best or against someone else who is further on in their journey is always a battle you will lose.

None of us are good at everything. Somethings we are better at and somethings we are worse at then others. So, when you're comparing against someone, you are putting your average against someone else's best. No wonder you're going to feel shitty.

You end up resenting others for doing well, even when you don't really know a person or what they have gone through. Your efforts end up going into either keeping up with said person or trying to knock them down. Neither of which is beneficial to you or health.

It's not a 'competition' you can ever really win or one you will gain from. Even if you do feel like you're 'winning'. It's a temporary feeling and you will soon find someone else to feel inferior to.

Stop competing with others, put your scorecards away.

The only person you should be comparing yourself against is yourself. It sounds so cliché I know but there is no one else who can do you better then you.

No one can ever be as good at being you. This is the only game you are ever going to truly win. When you start thinking like this. The pressures of trying to be someone else or fitting another mold are lifted.

Your entire focus can then be to concentrate on solely improving yourself to be a better you.

The point is you should be better than you are but not because you're worse than other people but because you're not everything you know you should be.

When you stop focusing on other people and focus on yourself, only then do you start getting a better idea of what actually matters. That is, you!

Figure out your strengths, what you're great at, what you enjoy doing the most. Then go all in on that. Aim for nothing less than self-love and happiness within. Why try to be the 2nd, 3rd or 48th version of someone else and do it poorly when you can be the one and only version of yourself and it do it fan-fucking-tastically.

11. Natalie Suzanne

Now the title of this chapter is interesting. The chapter title was 'Accountability' but I renamed it.

The reason why, I will explain within this chapter.

Many months ago I got a bit worried that I was sharing all my experiences of Self Development and self-belief on Social Media.....but worried that It was just being watched. I was just a piece of content that helped my followers pass a poo or something to watch while they're at work looking to kill time.

While I am fully aware that that is true for 80% of my followers. I wanted to ensure what I was doing on my social was actually making a difference. That what I was sharing was actually helping.

Without a truly accurate way of being to be able to measure this, I decided to start an open challenge to all my followers.

The challenge was the 'Be A Shark Challenge'.

The challenge lasted for a month and the purpose was to help the people taking part move forward. To help them be more accountable, to understand their 'why', to get them outside their comfort zones, to set themselves goals and to really keep on top of them for a month. Even just being someone available to go 'hey how are you getting on'.

I had ten people take part in the challenge (1 would have made this challenge worthwhile so 10 was plenty)

Out of the 10 who took part. 8 took action.

Some of the goals included weight loss, completing outstanding work, keeping up with new work, new habits and just getting the shit that had been put off for too long, done! I also took part in the challenge myself and my personal target was to sleep more.

Now the first part of the challenge and the most important part. Was the **Declaration**! Now I put that word in bold because that it is one of the most important parts of being accountable.

Declaration - a formal or explicit statement or announcement.

This is what you are going to hold yourself against. This is what you're measuring up to. Without a declaration you have no start line. You have no promise to yourself and you can stop the challenge at any time and feel no inner judgement.

HOWEVER!

With a declaration......you have it hanging over you, you have a reason why and you have immediate pressure and while an internal declaration is one thing a Public declaration is some next level shit!

The main reason why it sticks more.... when you declare publicly to multiple people that you are going to do something....you will work a lot harder because if you don't achieve it....you will look like a dick. Nobody wants to look like a dick!

So, this was the first part of the challenge. I got all the challenge participants to upload their declaration on Social Media to all their followers.

Now in truth, people don't really give a shit. They may go 'oh look so and so is saying they're going to do that' in a passing thought but that's about it. However, that doesn't stop you from thinking, my god I'm gonna look like a right prat if I say I am going to do this and don't.

Now the declaration was out of the way it was up to the participants to provide weekly updates. Once again publicly as well. One of the challenges was to also go on Video to update people on their progress.

Now to help push the participants I decided to pick a winner at the end of this. The winner would receive a 'Be A Shark' bundle which included a number of books, sweets, a whiteboard, an audible subscription and most importantly a chapter in my upcoming book named after them.

Here we are!

The main takeaway from this challenge.....action was taken!

2.4 Stone was lost in weight from the participants collectively, a theory test was booked, connections were made, goals were set. Heck It was during this challenge that I 'Declared' that I would be writing this book.

Also......a certain individual named 'Natalie Suzanne' worked towards conquering a phobia.

Natalie Suzanne suffers from a condition called Agoraphobia.

Agoraphobia is a type of anxiety disorder in which you fear and avoid places or situations that might cause you to panic and make you feel trapped, helpless or embarrassed. It is a crippling condition.

A condition which has prevented Natalie from leaving her house, whether that means going out of for a short walk or even a drive.

During this challenge.... Natalie.... did both..... multiple times.

She took her little legend of sausage dog 'the legend' known as Patrick on walks, bearing awful weather and got back behind a wheel of a car.

She always went above and beyond and documented her progress with multiple videos discussing here progress and sharing her journey with others.

Natalie inspired me during the challenge and even pushed me. It was for this reason she won the challenge and it was for this reason she rightfully has a chapter named after her in this book.

Well done to Natalie. Remember this, you have more strength than most and you truly are a Sharky bastard!

Accountability is without doubt is the most underestimated part of self-development.

If you want a hack to achieve more and get more shit done. Accountability is it. Whenever I want to get something done. I get out my phone, create a public declaration, set and date and that's it.

I always achieve it.....quite simply because I don't wanna look like a dick and it's a great feeling to do something they you say you're going to do.

There is no kick up the arse like having an audience to see if you follow through.

It's not even whether you complete the objective or not, it's more about having the integrity of attempting what you said you would.

You may be thinking, well what's the point if I'm not even going to achieve it..... well an attempt is growth; an attempt is you pushing yourself and an attempt is more than most do.

If there is something you have been meaning to do or something you want to achieve. Declare it. Tell someone.....make it real.

This doesn't have to be public. This can be with a close friend, partner or relative.....but you must share it!

If 'not looking like a dick' is not enough of an incentive. Put something else against it. Buy yourself something guilt free if you achieve this by this. Get a loved one to promise you something if you hold up your end to the bargain.

When you don't declare it, you can say to yourself you're doing it Monday and then give up Tuesday and don't have to feel guilty or judge yourself......which sure that's great in the short term.....but holds back growth.....and only ensures the same repeatable start stop mentality. An endless loop of inner disappointment leading you nowhere.
Make it real, make it known and get it done.

Some other honourable mentions who partook in the Be A Shark Challenge:

Ell Shroff,
Elli Bows,
Finn Stubbings,
Laura Campbell,
Lisa Bennett,
Rikki Payne,
Sarah Collier

Well done, you sharky bunch of bastards!

12. Integrity

The way we feel about ourselves is another integral part of achieving success. Without inner integrity we are our own worst enemy. We can hold so much self-judgement that we may begin to feel that rewards are not deserved and we are just not capable of achieving them.

This may sound like a lack of confidence but inner confidence won't come without integrity, and without integrity any confidence we do gather is incredibly short-lived or feels put on like an act.

With inner integrity, you understand yourself worth. You know what you are capable of and know what you deserve. It's the difference between holding your head up high and proud of yourself or keeping your head down with guilt and not pushing for more.

It is the true way that Karma works.

Karma - the sum of a person's actions in this and previous states of existence, viewed as deciding their fate in future existences.

Quite simply, you do good, you get rewarded in life. You do bad, bad things will happen.

However, I don't see this as something spiritual. I see it as common sense. When you do something shitty, you put a dent in your integrity. You end up feeling shitty about yourself. You do something good; you get a little buzz; a little lift and you then start to feel good about yourself. There is no higher power or anything spiritual that does this. That is just the simple dynamics of it.

If you perform any task with confidence or with self-belief, the chances of you performing that task well are high, you may even over achieve. Compared to trying to complete a task while feeling sh*tty about ourselves, low confidence and self-doubt. Chances are you will not perform the task to your capabilities.

We all have a set of moral values, a code that we know we shouldn't compromise. We shouldn't lie, we shouldn't cheat and we shouldn't steal etc. We know what is wrong and we know what will make us feel shitty.

When we do compromise on our inner values we chip away at our inner integrity.

Say for instance you steal something. You took some money off someone. You have gained temporarily. You have gained money. You may off needed that money because you wanted something that you can now buy. You may try to condone your action by telling yourself, 'the person you stole from didn't need the money; they may not have even noticed it going missing'. Great you now have the money. You feel great.... temporarily. What you have also done is sacrificed a small part of your integrity.

Another example is you may intentionally go out of your way to belittle someone. Not necessarily bullying but going out of your way to make yourself feel superior over someone else at their expense. Yes, you may feel good for a moment. Puff out your chest and feel all proud of yourself because 'you showed them' but if you keep doing it you will soon realise that when thinking of that person, you may guilt.

One other example would by lying. Often the main reason we lie is to avoid the pain and torment that may come alongside telling the truth. To avoid the initial confrontation. Again, short term you may feel that you've 'dodged a bullet' and feel relief. However, when you have to hold on to a lie, the burden of it grows stronger. Your inner integrity diminishes the longer you hold it.

The lie becomes bigger and bigger, bigger than what it ever was before. You begin telling more lies to cover your lies. Pointless little lies that keep you out of enough trouble for the moment. The initial pain and torment that you initially avoided at the beginning ends up coming back tenfold.

Now this is all without being caught or found out. Even if you did manage to get away with stealing or lying. Your own image of yourself is in tatters. You have surrendered a slither of self-respect for a small temporary gain.

The thoughts you tell yourself are……. you're a thief, you're a liar or you're a cheat. You don't deserve this opportunity. You don't deserve to have friends like these. You also know something is coming around the corner to bite you in the arse. This isn't karma coming back round to get you. That is you, you feeling so shitty about yourself that you continue to make the bad choices rather than the good. Self sabotage.

You begin to feel like a bad person rather than a good one. Feelings of guilt arise from betraying your own rules and core values.

You do not wake up one morning a bad person. It happens by a thousand tiny surrenders of self-respect and self-interest.

We are human beings we are always going to make mistakes; we are always going to lie, we are always going to take something that we don't feel like we deserve. Nobody doesn't, but it's about tipping the scales towards making the right choices more often than the bad ones.

Even if you know you're never going to get caught or found out. When we do the right things and keep our integrity, life becomes a lot simpler. We prevent this inner critic questioning ourselves and we live a life with nothing to hide, being able to sleep comfortably each night.

You have an inclination subconsciously of what is right and was is wrong. Think about what you want to be known by? Being someone who is honest, reliable? Set you're values and then always try to adhere to them. Keep your integrity.

Doing the right things even when no one is watching, even when we know no one will ever know is a sign of true inner integrity. Integrity is a choice we make, and it's a choice we must keep making throughout most moments of our lives.

Guilt

Guilt is the one emotion we should look to eradicate. Holding it unnecessarily strengthens our inner critic.

You could argue that guilt is a good emotion because it prevents you from making the same mistake twice however once you have made a mistake and corrected your current values, learnt the lesson..... why keep punishing yourself by holding onto the emotion of guilt.

We need to learn to forgive ourselves more, make the necessary alterations to who we are, to our character and our values to ensure we prevent the previous mistakes from happening but certainly not keep hold of the judgement.

Holding onto the guilt doesn't prevent the past. It ensures the past keeps a hold of you.

Living in the past is like driving down the road in reverse. You can drive in reverse, being fully dependent on your rear-view mirror to navigate. You can drive but your chances of comfortable and smooth journey where you will go far are slim.

Appreciate your past is no longer a reflection of who you are now and concentrate on who you are now in the present.

Instead of holding on negatively, appreciate your past and the lessons you've learnt because they have made you who you are now and prevent you from future mistakes.

Self-Judgement

Many people have this belief that those who are successful inevitably feel good about themselves all the time and are free from self-doubt and insecurities.

Judgment is a human condition. EVERYONE judges themself.

There is always the self-critic inside you questioning every step you make, every decision you make.

Think of it as a piece of software. This piece of software has been programmed throughout your lifetime. Your parents began writing it. Your friends, your teachers had part to play and you are at the helm constantly entering data into this programme.

Every mistake you make, every emotion you have felt and every experience has gone into this programme called 'The Inner Critic'

The purpose of the programme is to ensure nothing but survival, it's holding your best interest at heart. It is also the harshest and most honest critic you will meet. It doesn't hold any punches and will criticise and question you more than anyone you will ever meet.

This programme often goes unnoticed and people just play along to what their subconscious tells them to do. We are often unaware that it sits quietly, constantly impacting every decision we make.

What you will tend to find is the people who have a good self-worth, high levels of success and who seem to have everything together. They still have the self-doubts, they still question themselves, but they have a better relationship with their 'Inner Critic'

Just like your parents who have your best interests at heart, it is ok to questions their advice and criticism. You mum may not want you to ride a motorcycle, it doesn't mean you shouldn't ride one. Your mum, just like your inner critic, is looking out for you. If you listened and did what your parents or teachers told you all the time life would be pretty f*cking boring.

When this inner critic does pop into your head telling you......"you can't do this", "you shouldn't do that". Question it. Ask yourself, does this bit of advice and self-judgement serve you?
Even ignore it. Be aware that these types of thoughts will come up as they are part of your programming and it is ok to let them pass.

Don't give it any weight. They more time you spend not listening to the critic, the more your programming adjusts. So, the inner critic eventually stops raising the same questions and doubts when you want to attempt something. Limitations are removed and self-doubt reduces.

Spend a few moments next time a self-judgement thought pops in your head to identify it. Question it and think of how beneficial it would be to ignore it.

Appreciate that these negative thoughts are temporary. Like a passing rain cloud in the sky, that comes and goes. You don't spend the day concentrating on the rain cloud that went overhead do you? So why hold onto these negatives thoughts that appear just as frequently?

We can often be our own worst enemy. Imagine how liberating it would be to be your own biggest fan.

The narrative we tell ourselves, the thoughts we concentrate on are so important. If we listen to the thoughts of self-doubt, that tell us we aren't good enough, that we are average, then you will be average. If you concentrate on the thoughts that everyone else is against you, that you're a victim. Then you will be a victim.

Change the narrative. When you learn to be aware of your inner arsehole (your 'inner critic') then we can take control and take charge of it. You can then concentrate on telling yourself a different story. One where you are the hero, you have massive importance in the world and the only limitations we have are the ones we give to ourselves.

13. Social Media

The introduction of social media over the last 10-15 Years has introduced a new wave of mental health issues.

On face value, social media can be a good way to feel connected with distant friends or a way to make new friends entirely.

However, so many people hold their self-value against their Social media profiles nowadays. Basing their worth on the number of likes their post got, the level of engagement and the comments people were leaving behind.

This has left people feeling anxious about posting anything at all. Feeling judged and comparing themselves to everything they see on their news feeds or stories.

Social Media is now a huge part of our life's and I want to dedicate this chapter on how to have a better relationship with it. So, you no longer fear it or the power (you think) it has over you.

Social Media is not a monster

So many people nowadays see social media as this evil monster. A monster that spreads hate, consumes attention and damages your mental health.

This isn't social medias fault, social media warps minds just as much as magazines did when they first came out. I'm sure there was an adjustment shift when people first saw pictures in a magazine. Same again with Radio, the ability to hear others people's opinion and news from people around the world.

Then again with TV and videos. Heck I know a lot of my personality and sense of humour are based on a lot of films I watched growing up.

Point being, with each couple of generations there is this new evil "monster" that society has to adjust to.

Is social media a monster? Are TV shows and movies a monster? Or is it something that society are still struggling to get to grips with?

Pinch of Salt

Understand a lot of what you see is not reality. So much content on social media is fake. Whether that is outrageous click bait articles. The village idiots scaremongering about 5G and the science behind why we shouldn't be wearing a mask or people's 'living their best life' pictures. Always remember there are a lot of sad and lonely people behind smiles on social media.

Catfishing is definitely on the rise as well. The amount of adjustments people can apply. With an apps like Facetune you can practically change and perfect your whole appearance within seconds. Changing your entire face and/or body to fit what you think is 'Social Media' worthy

Never take what you see or read as 'gospel', social media can be used to mask a lot of people's real-life problems. It's very easy to lose perspective on what is or isn't real.

Allocate your time

Now the reason I think Social Media is a tougher pill to swallow, compared to TV and magazines is because it provides soooooo much data at an instance. With a quick scroll of your thumb you can consume up 5-10 snapshots of data in a matter of seconds.

That is a lot of data to consume and a lot for our minds to process.

Limiting your time on social media will only benefit you. I think all of us could agree we have dedicated more time on social media then we would like. No one can be blamed. It's so easy to fall into a YouTube rabbit hole or a TikTok frenzy. Give your mind a break from absorbing so much information at once. Use apps that measure your screen time and monitor and manage your usage.

Productivity and focus

It takes a very strong person to see their phone ping and not take a glance or at worst pick up their phone. It's quite sad really but we react to pings on phones the same way dogs to treats. Ears up, tails wagging.

It's very easy to lose concentration and dedicate attention to your phone rather than your task at hand.

It's amazing how much more you get done by turning off your notifications on your phone. Without those constant interruptions or nudges

As mentioned, reducing your time on social media will gain back perspective not only on real life but what you bring to the table.

Watching others and comparing against what you see online, allows you quickly lose perspective on yourself and what values you offer. Take time out to reclaim a sense of self.

It's a lot easier to manage your time on social media with new settings on phones that help you dedicate a certain amount of time per day. Turn off those notifications. Let you dictate your time on social media rather than social media dictating it for us.

Don't care

Posting a picture or a video can be a daunting task to some. The idea that the content they post will be judged by a rath of people on social media can be enough to prevent anyone from posting.

Yes people may quickly glance at your video or photo, they may have a positive or negative thought.....and then they move on.

In truth though, no one really cares what you post. No one cares that much to sit and stare at it for hours. To share it with their friends to belittle or pick apart gossiping about you. That's your ego making up stories.

In the same way no one looks at your inspirational post and have it change their life. All your posts truly do is capture a few seconds of someone's attention and then it's forgotten.

They may gather a negative comment, but even that will be a throw away one.

I hate the thought of people only posting content to please others, to dodge judgement or garner engagement. Pandering for a like. Trying to please other people. It's your social media. Post whatever the fuck you want.

If you find yourself deleting posts because you no longer feel the post is good enough, this should ring alarm bells that you're reflecting your insecurities onto your social media.

The insecurity you feel with having an image up.... will only grow when you decide to delete it. All because you sat and stared at it for 30 minutes and decided that you actually think you're uglier then you originally thought when barely anyone has given it more then 10 seconds notice.

As an experiment I posted a picture of a crisp packet on my social media with the caption 'No Context'....... the world didn't end, I didn't lose or gain followers, no one cared....and somehow it even got 5 likes.

Do Not Delete......Stop Caring too much because no one else does.

Be F*cking You

Its sound so basic and a simple request. It is far too easy to fake things on social media. Whether that be posing by a fancy car that isn't yours, photoshopping your image to make yourself look more Kardashian.

There is a piece of an empty airplane with three rows of seats, a window and some green screen in a studio you can rent for £50, just so you can get a snap of you on a Private jet!?! That's the lengths people will go to, to make things appear better than they are.

It's not that difficult to bullshit people, but people have gotten a lot savvier when it comes to spotting bullshit.

You are not going to have a good or healthy time not being yourself on Social Media. This will lead you down a path of loneliness.

People will not resonate or trust you on social media unless you are being yourself.

Don't be a prune and shy away from showing off yourself, for celebrating you and what you're about. Don't hold back.

If people unfollow you for you truly being yourself, celebrate it. They are not part of your tribe and you no longer have to waste time pandering to them.

What you will be left with are authentic followers who truly know you and who want to celebrate you and all your success.

Be Vulnerable, be authentic and Be Fucking You!

No Right and wrong

Stop worrying about Judgement, worrying about opinions, again……no one fucking cares! There is no right or wrong way of doing social media. You can use it in any way you want.

Improve your relationship

There are a number of things I would suggest you avoid to have a better relationship with yourself and with social media.

1. **Tricking the system.**

Don't try to hack things, don't try to manipulate the platform to gain more engagement or more followers. Do not buy followers…..I did this in the past and although your number of followers grow……..it leaves you with thousands of people who don't give and shit and won't engage with you. You would feel like a bit of a knob if you went on a night out and paid a load of people to pretend to be your friend.

Also the site I found for buying the followers was a bit pokey, I'm pretty sure I inadvertently funded ISIS

2. Don't delete

Just don't do it, if you look at an image or video of yourself and it's making you a bit 'anxious'……. don't fucking delete. You will give in to that insecurity and your 'anxiety' will grow even worse for next time. Own it and keep it! End off!

3. Photoshop/Facetune

Remove these for fuck sake. Delete the app.

Giving yourself plastic surgery on every picture you take is setting yourself an unrealistic standard that you don't need to live by. News flash, It's so embarrassingly obvious as well. Like really obvious!

I have seen so many people's post in the morning and then seen them later on the day and you think wow, did you get run over on the way here or something?

Stop hiding spots, stop whitening teeth, stop giving yourself extra or less curves. Be you, be normal and celebrate what you got.

4. Concentrating on the numbers

The number of followers does not determine you or your progress on Social Media. People get disheartened for only having a few 100 followers on Instagram. Don't!

I would rather have 100 followers who follow me for me, engage with me then have 10,000 strangers who couldn't give a shit and don't know you for who you truly are.

Do not let an unfollow dishearten you. I know plenty of individuals who have closed their accounts or put their accounts on hold to help with their own anxiety. They have closed their account for themselves.

Somebody else, someone who used to be followed by them may notice their follower number has gone down by one and judge themselves as if they have caused this. Question their last post.

Even If someone did unfollow you because they didn't like your content. Good, one less person to pander to, one less person who will reap the benefits of you. I would much rather an unfollow then someone who keeps following me so they can sit there and silently hate on me.

Sharing a message, even if 10 people see it is still powerful and shouldn't be underestimated.

Imagine ten people in a room actively listening to you. Stop expecting to only share a message or promote your business when you have thousands of followers. It's with your consistency and authenticity that you get there.

Stop seeing social media as a hindrance and work out a way to make it work for you. We get to live in a time that we get to use social media as a tool.

Engage, Encourage and Enlighten others.

14. Change

Now many people are unhappy with their current circumstance. There will be something about themselves or something about their situation, that if they could, they would change in an instant.

They're not happy with the job they're in, they're not happy with their weight. They're not happy with the way they're are being treated. They're not happy with how they feel about themselves.

If you are unhappy with your current situation, you feel like whatever you do, nothing is really changing and you keep getting the same negative results. You're probably doing the same things over and over and getting the same results.

If you continue to do the same things and if you continue to stay on your current course it's unlikely anything is going to change. You're going to see the same old results.

Something needs to change because whatever you're doing now......obviously isn't working.

People often want drastic lifestyle changes or drastic weight loss. If you want drastic change, you have to change drastically.

You need to stop expecting things to change for you and for something new to just eventually land in your lap. The things that you think will happen at 'some point down the line'.....don't! Not without change or some sort of action.

Why wait for something new to enter your life when you could implement the change and expedite the new path now?

Change is necessary throughout life. Change brings with it new opportunities and experiences. It ensures that life stays exciting. Change helps you move on; it helps you progress.

It is often feared as it gets you out of your comfort zone. It puts you into the unknown. However, when you allow yourself to change, adapt and grow, you open the door to a fuller life and a more fruitful future.

Change will inevitable come, it's part of life and its often forced on you. Somebody passes away or you get made redundant, I mean COVID ffs! etc but to be better prepared for these unexpected events we should seek change often.

Keep things fresh and exciting, keep yourself on your toes. It can be a change of job, a change of environment like where you live or where you get your coffee, each morning or even taking a different route to work.

When you apply change often, it is you who is in control. You are prepared for what life has to through at you and you're ready to adapt and roll with the punches for when the changes life throw at you eventually come.

Of course, with every change there is an element of risk. However, the risk that comes with change is where the growth comes from.

When you really stop and think about change and the risk that comes with it. It is easy for your autopilot to fill your head with 800 reasons why you shouldn't do something. Now if you stop and take a moment to analysis these fears.....are any of them actually true.

Let's say for instance, you've always wanted to jump out of a plane? A sky dive. If you stop and think about it.....it can come across as pretty f*cking stupid idea!

Jumping out of a moving plane at 14,000 feet, plunging towards the surface of the earth at 130mph with the only chance of survival is being strapped to some stranger who you have only just met, hoping that the guy has had a good day so far! The idea can seem pretty fucking daft.

The thoughts don't stop there. You end up down a rabbit hole of thoughtful quivers......this bloke who you're strapped to, even on his best day is still dependent on a sheet of nylon!

Someone can be forgiven for not wanting to go ahead with the idea. BUT! Get yourself comfortable with the worst scenario. Ask yourself. What is the worst that could happen? The worst that can happen.....you could die. Obviously not an ideal outcome but heck, it will be over in a flash and at least you go out on your sword. There are fewer noble ways to go. Elvis died overweight on a toilet FFS and that guy was a king.

Why miss out on one of life's thrilling experiences because of over the top stories you tell yourself.
Once you get comfortable with the worst outcome the fear diminishes.

Do not fear change, change your fears.

15. The Ignition

So, this is it, this is potential the chapter that will ignite that little fire, give you the literal kick up the ass you require to get started.

Before we get going, remember this. You win at everything you do. Sounds like a cheesy Instagram quote doesn't it, but you really do, you can literally do anything you put your mind to.

Unfortunately, you put your mind to the predicted failures. You put your mind to your toured past, your poor upbringing. You think about not being able to do it therefore you don't do it. You have proved yourself correct.

Therefore, making you a massive winner.

We go out of our way, above and beyond to prove ourselves correct. If you think you won't be able to get started....you won't get started......winning! You done it; you did what you set your mind to! Congratulations!

You have convinced yourself you're unlovable, no one can ever put up with you.....wow what a winner, look how single you are!

You're adamant you're incapable of losing weight.....wow well done you, what's that......you're gaining more weight? Somebody give you a medal!

You see how you can be your biggest worst enemy? The messages you're telling yourself come true. Today.....we change those messages.

Instead of 'I am incapable of love', it's 'you would be lucky to have me'.

Instead of 'I will fail as soon as I get started', it's 'I will overcome every obstacle I come across'.

Now we have your mind in the right direction, let's get going.

I Niall Macmillan, give you full and total permission to do what you want, I Niall MacMillan think it's a good idea to start your business idea, I Niall Macmillan think it's a good idea for you to travel or move to Australia or take a gap year. I Niall Macmillan give you permission to quit your job and try another career path. I Niall MacMillan give you permission to leave your other half who makes you miserable.

You see for a lot of us, we have the ideas, we know what we want to do but we almost sit and wait for permission to do something. Well there you go I am

giving it to you. Whatever your idea, I Niall MacMillan give you permission.
Just get started and just take action on all your ideas.

Everything I gave permission for above, what's the worst that's going to happen. You take action, you go for it, you can always go back.

If you move to Australia, worst case you can come back home.

If you start a new career, you can always go back to your old one.

If you leave your partner, you can always work to rekindle things.

Just promise me now you have permission to do it, make sure you DO it. I don't want you trying it.

Trying suggests its temporary. Doing it is having an open mind to endless possibilities.

In the words of the Star Wars Jedi Master Yoda, "Do or do not. There is no try."

Stop searching for certainty, stop trying to make sense out of everything and predicting the future.
When you stop trying to make sense out of everything all the stress you may hold.....melts away.

Life is adventure, it's meant to be lived, not controlled. Enjoy the struggles, embrace the obstacles and live for the journey.
Remember that it IS a journey, not a destination. Yes, you have a goal you want to accomplish, but you will learn and grow along the way and that is where the fun and fulfilment is. That is where the 'living' is.

Sometimes the process itself is the best experience, so don't stay so focused on the end goal that you miss the opportunity to enjoy the steps you take. Celebrate each and every step you take to keep your momentum.

If it's only about achieving the goal, you are likely to lose steam along the way. Take time to think about your actions today and today only.

A man a lot wiser than me had the following to say about living in the moment and says it best: "Yesterday is history, tomorrow is a mystery, today is a gift ... that's why we call it the Present."

So now were ready to get started make it real.

Write it down. Buy yourself a whiteboard of famazon right now. Don't think just do. Would you spend £10 to start taking action, would you spend £10 to have a clear idea of what you want in life? Would you spend £10 to clear your head space?

If you really are that tight there is a wonderful thing called paper or a notes app.

Write down in a statement what it is you want out of life. Really write it all down. Treat yourself, go crazy.

Once you have that list out of you head, chunk it down! Make it bitesize, what are actions you can take now that are a step towards your goal. Don't try and do it all at once and overwhelm yourself. One step at a time, one foot in front of the other.

You have everything you need right now to get started, you have a goal, you've made it real and you have a mobile phone. There is nothing else you need.

Don't hold back from starting because you haven't got this equipment, you haven't done this course, you don't have the correct tools.

A lot of people wait and spend £200.00 on gym gear before they go to the gym.

A photographer may think he needs a £800.00 camera before he starts a new photographer business.

It's all rubbish and it's a way of your mind keeping you from doing something uncertain.

JUST GET STARTED!

People often wait for that dose of motivation, to wait until the time is right or when they're feeling the best about themselves.

If we sit around waiting to be in the right mood, we'll never get started. If you depend on motivation to accomplish something then there is no point getting started. You need to act with or without feeling good.

We become by performing unmotivated action, relentless action. On our darkest day, we still take a step.

When you start to take action you soon build up a skill set, a resilience, where you take things on without hesitation, action becomes a habit because you know the thoughts during hesitation are the only things that will help you fail.

When you start taking action over thoughts, over opinions we start doing and we start living life, a life of fulfilment, of optimism.

Actions conquers doubt and fear. Action breeds confidence and courage.

Don't know what to do or where to start...

Good, that's your first action.....read a book, look online, ask for advice and do whatever you need to do. The next action after will appear, you will know what you need to do. You probably already know now.

Nothing is coming for you, no one is coming to save you or miraculous change your life. You have to start; it is on you and you have start now.
Here's a heads up, you won't see the rewards soon, not even within a year.

You will see glimpses or signs that you may have made the right decision but you won't be certain for years. There will be days where you question yourself. There will be days you don't feel like it. This is all natural, you're shocking your system, shocking yourself and what you know. But being the shark, you are going to become, you will hold relentlessness!

You will build a character and a mindset that even on a bad day, you turn up! That is not today though. Don't think that fair ahead. Don't give yourself a chance to question. Don't give yourself a chance to think. Don't give yourself a chance to feel.

Fuck how you feel, Just ACT!

16. The Toolkit

So, you have read the book. You now realise that you are responsible for your shit. You feel motivated, now you have to implement discipline. Great!

I am not naïve to the fact that this sudden burst of optimism will be short lived.

What happens when you don't feel like it and you can't over power your autopilot?

This chapter I want to be used as a quick reference point. A trouble-shooter if you will. Whenever you're not feeling 'sharky', visit this chapter and give it a quick read.

Self MOT

There are simple questions that you should ask yourself before you start thinking your world is crumbling all around you.

Before you start thinking the worst check the below. They are so simple but simple questions you need to ask yourself.

Have you had sleep?

Have you had a good 8-9-hour sleep in a while? Have you had a few late nights? Whenever I lose momentum or motivation....9/10 it is because of this.

I always make sure to have an early night or a few cheeky catch up naps. Sleep is so underrated and change a mindset instantly.

What have you eaten?

Have you had Vitamin rich or organic food recently? Or you suffering from a Dominoes hangover? Have a few days without processed food and see how quickly you adjust, how much energy you gain.

If you're suffering from a hangover and reading this. It goes without saying your body is craving excess sugars. Your body will be screaming for sugars that it thinks it needs. Ignore it and eat some good fuel. It will be over soon!

Fresh air?

When is the last time you were outside. I don't mean on the school run or taking the bins out. I mean properly outside getting some fresh air?

A lot of you may be reading this in lockdown. It can be quite easy to be stuck inside for days and days. Even being indoors for half a day can be enough for me. Go outside and get a few deep breaths. Put the phone down and enjoy the ambience.

Just take a moment to listen to all the background noise and have a few breaths. Shake off that cabin fever!

Exercise/Walk?

I'm not even talking about anything hard work. A minimum 15-20-minute walk all to yourself I would prescribe to everyone. Listen to music, listen to an audiobook, enjoy the silence. Get those steps in.

This has been the biggest helper for me in my self-development journey. Not even for cardiovascular benefits but the ideas I have come up with, the things I have thought out, the knowledge I have gained just from a daily dose of walking.

Implement more tasking exercise to multiple the benefits. I'm not gonna spend a few paragraphs talking about endorphins or the scientific benefits.

Just know you should look to make it part of your daily routines. If you feel lost now, or feel like shit. Have a 15-20-minute walk to yourself and see how much it can change the perspective of your day.

What are you wearing?

Provocative right? But seriously.... have you had a shower yet? Are you still in your pyjamas? You even wearing a bra. Guys have you done your hair? Simply showering, feeling clean and dressing up can do wonders for your mood. Stop laying around with a bad smell and treat yourself.

Talk it out?

Things on your mind? Have some stuff on your chest? There is a huge benefit of just saying what's on your mind out loud. Call your parents, call a best friend, call your partner......heck there are specific numbers you can call specifically for things like this. Even have a conversation with yourself.

Talk to yourself and ask why you think you're feeling the way that you do. You can quickly identify the reasons you're feeling down by just saying things out loud and no longer keeping it to yourself.

Social Media?

Have you seen something that's made you feel shitty online? Feeling low? Go on a mass unfollow or mute spree.

If something negatively triggers you in anyway.........Get it gone! Have a friend who constantly shares drama? Boom! Blocked! Don't allow drama or any sort of unnecessary negativity into your headspace.

Put up your social media force field and block/unfollow/mute the shit!

Overwhelmed?

Do you have a list of tasks that you're behind on? Do you have tight deadlines to meet? First of all, the list of tasks you have. Have you actually made them into a list or are they clogging up your headspace? No wonder you're overwhelmed.

Slap them on your notes, write them down into an actual list. Once you have them written get some of the smaller/easier tasks done. Starting small is getting started, that's the hardest part. Now you're started, go from there, build the momentum.

See how good you feel when your cross that thing of your list. Give yourself a little productivity boner and write that shit down!

Deflated?

You feel deflated, uninspired, bored? Book something! Treat yourself to something, something that will make you feel alive or something that will give you something to look forward to.

I'm almost 99.9% certain that if you're feeling a bit down in the dumps, you adhere to one of the above.

Know that you are not on your own. You have people around you who will be happy to help.

If you ever feel down, send me a message on Instagram. Never feel like you can't message. Don't question it. If you come to the end of this MOT and still struggling, ping me a message.

Think of me as your AA. Your RAC cover. If you really can't solve it and you have an emergency breakdown. Give me a message.

Instagram: @niallmacmillan

17. The Wrap Up

It's safe to say this book has been one of the hardest things I have ever done. I'm not a natural writer and I struggle to put my thoughts and practices into word format.

I also grossly underestimated the effort involved. I knew what I wanted to put down, I know it in my head but to translate it into a book was hard work.

Also, I have never truly understood the capabilities of Microsoft Word before. My God it has held my hand through this book writing journey. I predicted 6 months it has taken me 12!

I have had my own mental battles to keep chipping away at this book and have found for whatever reason I can only write it when I'm out of my house.

So, I would like to thank McDonalds, Costa, a few cafes and mainly my local gym for putting up with me at half 6 in the morning sitting silently in the corner of a dark room while I have written this.

There have been many times that I have woken up and thought I'll leave the book for today.

But It's always been a good kick up the arse when I have a conversation with myself internally on a cold groggy morning…..'ffs Niall come on, you're supposed to be writing a book about this stuff! Get moving!', It works a treat everytime.

I would like to think of this book as a little keepsake for my kids. To Mylie, Casey and Ellison. I'm sure you all will never read it but just in case you do. I love you all very much and you all make me so proud every day. You're the reason I do and try to achieve so much. I don't want to tell you what is possible, I want to show you. I'm setting that bar high!

I also want to thank my wife Lauren for somehow putting up with me. It can't be easy to have a husband who doesn't sit still and is always up to something. When I am off in the clouds you keep me centred.

It is with her belief that I have gotten to where I am today. While I'm constantly trying to help and support the people around me, she is the one who supports and who mentors me.

I also want to thank my parents. Knowing them and being a parent myself, I know they will feel guilty as if the didn't give me the upbringing they would of wanted. This couldn't be further from the truth.

My Dad is the most stoic and inspirational man I know and my mum couldn't be anymore of a number one fan if she tried. They have raised me full of self belief, self acceptance and empathy. I couldn't of been happier.

So, in closing. I have tried to remove any 'fluff' or 'padding' that you tend to find in books and just tried to cut right to it. This book is a repository of my self development journey and what I have learnt so far.

I hope that you have picked this book up and found something within it that has helped move you forward on your journey.
Whether it's been a helping hand on a down day or a necessary wake up call. Even a part in the book that just hit different.

The main thing I get from reading these types of books are 'f*ck me' we're all struggling, we all have down days, we all have these negative thoughts about ourselves'. Sometimes it can feel like its just you suffering.

I hope it's a friendly reminder that we are all the same and you're not on your own. We are all winging it. I know I am and so far, these are my findings and what have helped me. I hope they have helped you.

Lets all work together, to push each other but most importantly by pushing ourselves.

Don't settle and strive for more!

Take Your Place, Leave Your Mark, Live Your Life & Be a Shark

Printed in Great Britain
by Amazon

67741655R00071